D0450091

THE WORLD OF HARLEY-DAVIDSON

HARLEY-
DAVIDSON

THE WORLD OF HARLEY-DAVIDSON

TOM ISITT

First published in 1992 by
Bison Books Ltd
Kimbolton House
117A Fulham Road
London SW3 6RL

ISBN 0-86124-930-5

Printed in China

Reprinted 1993
Reprinted 1994

Page 1: *The epitome of the Harley-Davidson spirit – two-up on the road and heading nowhere in particular. For many owners this is an integral part of the Harley experience.*

Pages 2-3: *A pristine example of one of Harley-Davidson's most distinctive and important models – the Knucklehead. This is a 1936 model 61-E, the first overhead valve Harley engine.*

Below: *The archetypal Harley chop of the 1970s. This one uses a Panhead engine in a hardtail chassis with a raked-out front end. Modern customizing has forsaken this style in favor of the more traditional retro-look.*

Below right: *This much-cherished FLH Electra Glide, while not exactly original, shows the lengths to which some will go to make their Harleys stand out in a crowd. White leather tassels may not be to everyone's taste, but they certainly look distinctive.*

CONTENTS

PFB
418Y

THE LEGEND

The Harley-Davidson is a legend. That's not a matter of opinion, it's an indisputable fact. Ask anyone to name a famous make of motorcycle and they're almost certain to say 'Harley-Davidson'. Mention Harley-Davidsons to most people and they will conjure up in their minds a variety of images from Hell's Angels to California Highway Patrolmen, from latter-day cowboys to Hollywood paperazzi. In the 80 or so years that Harleys have been in production they have become the very symbol of American values. Harleys are synonymous with patriotism, freedom and the American Dream.

The transition of the Harley from mere motorcycle to the stuff that dreams are made of is difficult to pinpoint. It wasn't really until after World War Two, when most of the remaining motorcycle manufacturers in the USA had gone to the wall, that the Harley began its rise to stardom. At that point the Harley developed two completely separate images. Many GIs returned from the war unable to adapt to civilian life, and formed outlaw biker gangs aboard their war-surplus Harley-Davidsons. The incident at Hollister in 1947, upon which the film *The Wild One* was based, spawned the legend of the beer-swilling, brawling Harley-rider. While Brando did not ride a Harley in *The Wild One*, Lee Marvin did, and this was the first of many movies to portray the Harley as a mount for hell-raising bad boys.

Meanwhile, the Harley, with its patriotic image, was fast becoming the chosen plaything of the Hollywood stars. Many celebrities followed in the footsteps of Harley-riding Clark Gable. Suddenly they were all at it. Harleys could be found in the garages of the rich and famous all over America and it seemed that anyone with a macho-American image to support had to have a Harley tucked away somewhere.

But it was the late 1960s and early 1970s that saw the Harley gain real recognition as a cult icon. Films like *The Wild Angels, Easy Rider* and *Electra Glide in Blue* featured Harleys prominently. The celebrated documentary *On Any Sunday* went some way to cleaning up the image of Harley-Davidsons by following the exploits of Mert Lawill, Harley-Davidson's factory rider in the AMA championship, but the image of the rebellious Harley rider remained. While you might meet the nicest people on a Honda, real men rode Harleys and were proud of it.

By the 1980s the Harley had become as much a status symbol as a symbol of rebellion. Harleys had never been cheap, but now that they were both expensive and user-friendly, anyone with the cash and the inclination could buy themselves what was now seen as a piece of history. Film stars and musicians fell over themselves to be seen on their Harleys, and it wasn't long before the advertising agencies caught on to the Harley as something that symbolized rebellion, but lacked all the inconveniences of real revolt. With people like Lou Reed, Billy Idol and Arnold Schwarzeneggar riding around on them, Harleys were now things to be seen on. The Harley, a quintessentially American motorcycle, was not only part of the American Dream, it was a fashion statement and an enduring legend.

Page 6: *The sun comes up over Harleys at Littlecote. This big Harley rally in England attracts visitors from all over Europe and is hosted by millionaire businessman Peter de Savary, himself an avid Harley-Davidson enthusiast.*

Page 7 above: *The sissy-bar says it all – 'Made in the USA, Established in 1903'. Patriotic and with a pedigree; two things that are dearest to Harley-Davidson's target audience.*

Page 7 below: *The Fat Boy takes retro styling into new areas. Bold styling and a traditional approach have taken Harley-Davidson to the top of the big-bikes sales charts in the US.*

Right: *En route to Sturgis 1990, the biggest Harley gathering of all time, the boys take time to work on their impressions of extras from* The Loveless.

ERS·POST OFFICE.
UNLEADED
UNLEADED
11P6354
4Y0458
11P6384

Above: *Life's a beach . . . two radical chops beside the seaside. Preposterous upswept fishtail exhausts, huge cissy-bars and ape-hanger handlebars typify the* Easy Rider *look. Many a good Knucklehead and Panhead has been lost for ever like this.*

Left: *Possibly the most famous name in motorcycling, the Electra Glide is the only bike to have a film,* Electra Glide in Blue, *named after it.*

Right: *The work that goes into some customizing jobs is almost beyond belief. This white and gold-plated Sturgis, a special to celebrate the 50th Sturgis rally, must have taken hundreds of hours to complete.*

STURGIS 50th
Handcrafted by CUSTOM CHROME
"For the love of the Sport!"
August 12, 1990
STURGIS, S.D.

Above: *Harley-Davidson – a bike for all the family. Here we have His and Hers Harleys. Harley riders come in all shapes and sizes, both sexes and of all ages. On a Harley just about anything goes, but the emphasis is on the freedom to go as you please.*

Above right: *Merchandising is a big money-spinner for Harley-Davidson. Special-edition beers are just a few of the items within the enormous range of official Harley-Davidson products that ranges from underwear to bar stools.*

Right: *So fierce is the pride in Harley-Davidson ownership that few riders will have anything to do with other makes, particularly Japanese ones. This sign is typical of those found at major Harley gatherings such as Daytona and Sturgis . . . it's no idle threat, either.*

Left: *With the film* Terminator 2 *featuring Arnold Schwarzenegger on a Harley Fat Boy, this particular model has come to epitomize all that is desirable about the Harley-Davidson. It has also meant an increase in Harley Fat Boys at trendy locations around the world.*

Below: *Another 1930s Knucklehead, this one in good original condition. These are now becoming quite rare and are commanding commensurately high prices.*

Above: *This much-restored and customized 1930s side-valve Harley features springer forks and a hand gear-change. These days Harley-Davidson still use springer forks on the Springer Softail, but the hand gear-change has gone.*

Right: *They say that no two Harleys are the same once they've left the showroom; plenty of additional chrome and personalized paint-jobs make each Harley distinctive and as individual as the owner.*

Century 21
CORN DOGS
PLUMBING

THE BIKES

The Harley-Davidson story started back in 1903, when William S Harley and Arthur Davidson built their first motorcycle in a shed in Milwaukee. Actually it was more of a motorized bicycle, but then they all were in those days. Although not originally intended for sale, the first Harley-Davidson fired the imagination of several enthusiasts of the internal combustion engine and two more were built in 1904. The following year eight bikes were built to order and the existing shed was abandoned in favor of a purpose-built factory. With increased space, production rocketed to 49 machines in 1906, 157 units in 1907 and over 3000 by 1910. Harley-Davidson had arrived.

Until 1909 all Harleys had been single-cylinder machines, but 1909 saw the introduction of Harley-Davidson's first 45-degree V-twin – the Model F, which was superseded by the Model J two years later. This was a configuration already being used by their competitors, but eventually Harley-Davidson were to make it their own. From 1912 onwards Bill Harley, the technological brains of the outfit, introduced a series of technical innovations – the first successful clutch, a kick-start mechanism and by 1915 an innovative three-speed transmission.

Demand soared around this time, not just for Harleys but for all motorized products, and Harley were riding on the crest of a wave. Their factory race team was sweeping all before it, and demand had never been higher. Production reached 28,189 units in 1920, only to crash the following year to 10,202 as tens of thousands of inexpensive, mass-produced Model-T Fords began to flood the market. More by luck than by judgment Harley-Davidson survived this dip in their fortunes, helped significantly by their healthy export figures. As things began to look up they launched the JD, a 74 cubic-inch (1200cc) V-twin, and the most significant new model since the Model J. This model continued almost unchanged until 1929, when it was replaced by the VL. Meanwhile, H-D also introduced their first 45 cubic-inch side-valve V-twin – the DL.

The Depression of the 1930s caused another major slump in Harley-Davidson's fortunes, reducing production to 3703 bikes in 1933. To make matters worse, the VLs turned out to be horribly unreliable. Everything seemed to be going terribly wrong for Harley-Davidson, but despite this they continued to launch new models and to improve existing technology. The 74 and 80 cubic-inch twins now featured full roller-bearing engines and styling which is still considered to be exceptional.

Perhaps the most significant event of the 1930s was the introduction of the 61-E – the 'Knucklehead' – in 1936. The first of the overhead valve big twins, the Knucklehead is the bike upon which all subsequent big twins would be based. This was considered to be a performance motorcycle and consequently gave Harley-Davidson a significant advantage over their rivals at Indian. Another interesting model of the 1930s was the Servi-Car, a strange three-wheeled device powered by a 45 cubic-inch engine that was designed for use by garages as a breakdown/recovery vehicle, or by postal workers and traffic cops.

With World War II came a significant up-turn in Harley-Davidson's fortunes. Between 1942 and 1945 H-D produced more than 88,000 motorcycles for the armed forces. Most of the bikes were 45 cubic-inch WLA models, renowned for their durability rather than their performance.

Immediately after the war shortages of materials meant no new models from H-D, but in 1948, a year after the demise of the Knucklehead engine in both its 61 and 74 cubic-inch guises, the 'Panhead' was launched. In 61 and 74 cubic-inch incarnations the new Panhead engine featured hydraulic valve lifters and aluminum-alloy heads. It was lighter, quieter and more reliable than the Knucklehead, even if it was not significantly more powerful.

The following year saw another giant leap forward for Harley-Davidson with the introduction of the telescopic front fork. Up to this point all Harleys had featured rigid-spring forks, but with the introduction of the Hydra-Glide (as it became known) ride quality and handling improved immeasurably. It was at this point that the Harley began its metamorphosis into a tour-

ing-oriented motorcycle as comfort began to take precedence over performance.

By now production was booming and more than 31,000 machines rolled out of the factory in 1948. But after the initial enthusiasm for the Panheads demand slumped, due mainly to the increasing competition from British manufacturers. While the Brits had plenty of sports machinery, Harley had nothing to match Triumph's Speed Twins. After a brief fling with their K Models, a stop-gap machine whose real merits were front and rear suspension rather than speed, Harley-Davidson brought out the Sportster in 1957. This was a radical change, and 35 years later the Sportster is still the most popular bike in Harley's range. It was a 54 cubic-inch engine that could finally show the sporting British machinery a thing or two: American bikers could once again hold up their heads with pride. The combination of increased power and decreased weight gave the Sportster instant appeal, an appeal that is still there today.

Meanwhile, the Panheads were still going strong, and the Duo-Glide, launched in 1958 with suspension at both ends, was the forerunner of the Electra Glide. At the beginning of the 1960s H-D embarked on a range of lightweight and middleweight machinery in conjunction with the Italian Aermacchi company, which aimed to offer more variety in H-D's range. Needless to say they did not prove popular with a capacity-hungry public.

The first Electra Glide (so called because of its electric starter), was introduced in 1965 and the following year saw the end of the Panhead engine and the introduction of the Shovelhead. It had more power than the Panhead and proved very popular with the touring crowd. By the early 1970s the customizing scene was really taking off and Harley-Davidson, keen to cash-in on it, began to offer a series of 'factory customs' starting with the 1971 Super Glide. By this time Harley-Davidson had been taken over by the giant AMF corporation who were hoping to drag H-D into the latter-half of the 20th century. New production targets meant a drastic drop in quality control, while imports from Japan increased at an alarming rate.

The 1970s were a lean time at Harley. The Japanese were deluging the market with better quality products at lower prices, and AMF were beginning to regret having bought Harley-Davidson. Finally AMF offered the company to the management in 1981, took the money, and ran. This left Harley-Davidson facing a cold, harsh world alone. After successfully petitioning for import tariffs to give them some breathing space, H-D eventually produced a completely new range of alloy engines – the Evolution range – in 1983. It was the dawn of a new, and very successful era for Harley-Davidson. Quality control and reliability improved immeasurably, prices were competitive and suddenly they couldn't make enough of them. Apart from the new and much improved Sportsters, the big twins got five-speed gearboxes, belt drive and isolation-mounted engines. Softails and Low Riders became very desirable and by the mid-1980s Harley-Davidson was well and truly back.

Page 16: *Main Street at Sturgis, South Dakota. In amongst the thousands of bikes you will find every type of Harley-Davidson from the earliest side-valve V-twins to the very latest Dyna Glides. It doesn't matter whether it's a fully-dressed Tour Glide or a street legal XR750, as long as it's a Harley.*

Page 17: *An example of an early big cubic-inch twin, this early 1920s Harley would have cost under $400 new. Now it's worth more than twenty times that amount.*

Above left: *Early Harleys had a style all of their own. This one is a 1915 61 cubic-inch J-model in original trim and specification. Not the fastest or most comfortable of machines, it was nonetheless a very popular bike in its time.*

Above: *Although times have changed and automotive engineering has progressed, the essential appeal of the Harley is in a V-twin engine that was developed 70 years ago. This is a recent FLT Heritage Softail that uses an 80 cubic-inch (1340cc) Evolution engine and which is equipped with factory extras as befits a bike of this retro-styling.*

CXL 293
PI 3596
HARLEY-DAVIDSON
HARLEY-DAVIDSON
HARLEY-DAVIDSON
118

Left: *The 74 cubic-inch VL was hailed as the greatest achievement in motorcycling history when it was launched in the early 1930s, but it suffered terrible reliability problems.*

Below left: *The 45 cubic-inch side-valve engine was around for over 20 years from the late 1920s to the early 1950s. It formed the basis of the military WLAs and they were so rugged and reliable that there are a lot of them still running today.*

Above right: *The Knucklehead engine, in 61 and 74 cubic-inch capacities, was built between the early 1930s and the late 1940s. It was a performance motorcycle with overhead valves and proved both fast and popular.*

Below: *The Servi-Car, using the 45 cubic-inch side-valve motor, was used by meter maids, post office employees, garages and other small businesses for deliveries and was in production for over 40 years. There was a 74 cubic-inch prototype developed, but it was never put into production.*

Left: *An excellent example of an early 1940s 45 cubic-inch army-issue WLA. Harley-Davidson made over 80,000 such bikes for the Allied war effort and although they weren't very fast, they lasted a long time and were easy to fix – an important consideration when you're 5000 miles from your nearest Harley dealer.*

Left: *Not exactly the height of understated elegance, this immaculate 1965 FLH Electra Glide was one of the last Panhead motors. Many would say that the Panhead motor is the most aesthetically pleasing Harley engine, and it is this that makes them so popular on the customizing scene.*

Right: *The very latest Harley-Davidson to come out of the factory, the 80 cubic-inch Daytona. Produced to celebrate 50 years of Daytona Speed Week it incorporates the big Evolution engine in a Dyna-Glide chassis which uses a new rubber engine mounting system.*

Far left: *This fabulous Hydra-Glide was the first Harley-Davidson to use telescopic forks and the Panhead motor which replaced the Knucklehead. It is probably one of the best-looking Harleys ever made and now the model on which many specialist customizers base their retro creations.*

Left: *A closer look at the tank and instruments of the Hydra-Glide – simple, yet extremely elegant.*

Right: *In the 1960s Harley-Davidson signed a deal with the Italian Aermacchi company to produce small-capacity motorcycles. They sold quite well but were not popular with the traditional Harley fans. This is a slightly modified Ala Verde (although it is predominently red) 250cc Sprint.*

Right: *Some very serious restoration and chrome work has gone into this pristine Panhead engine. To some it may be a little over the top, but to your average Harley owner there's no such thing. Whether this particular example goes out in bad weather seems doubtful.*

PEACEMAKER

THE CUSTOMS

Almost since Harleys started to roll off the production line in significant numbers owners have customized their machines. As early as the 1920s Harley dealers stocked extensive ranges of after-market accessories, and nowadays the after-market and custom scene is huge. It is claimed that no two Harleys are identical, and you'd be hard pushed to find any two outside a dealer's showroom that are.

The custom scene really took off in the mid-1960s when choppers became all the rage. The idea was to make your bike look as lean and mean as possible by throwing away a lot of the extraneous and weighty parts and equipping it with extended forks and high handlebars. Many a good Harley was lost forever by this practice and the abomination ridden by Peter Fonda in *Easy Rider* is typical of this sort of customizing. Fortunately this habit has mostly disappeared, replaced instead by a custom scene mimicking Harleys from the '30s, '40s and '50s. Retro-customizing is now where it's at.

Customizing these days can really be split into two separate categories: 'aesthetic customizing' and 'performance customizing'. No one wants a bike that looks just like everyone else's, so most Harley owners spend varying amounts of time and money making theirs different. Aesthetic customizing usually comes in the form of bolt-on accessories, extra chrome and fancy paintwork. Some people will go as far as engraving engine cases and fork legs, but most content themselves with paint, chrome and bolt-ons. And for some people there is no such thing as too much chrome or too many running lights. The official Harley catalogs contain an enormous variety of bolt-on goodies – windshields, chromed casings, sissy bars, solo saddles, exhaust systems, lights, saddlebags; you name it, Harley offer it as an extra.

At the other end of the custom scene are the performance freaks. There are those who will say that trying to make a Harley go fast or handle well is a waste of time and money, but Harley-Davidson's *Screamin' Eagle* and *Eagle Iron* accessory catalogs are crammed with performance products designed to boost power,

sharpen up handling or improve braking. From performance carburetors to high-lift cams, it's all there in the Harley catalog.

Whether all this is the height of good taste or the last word in kitsch depends very much on your viewpoint. To some, a fully-dressed purple Tour Glide with every conceivable extra, a mink-covered King and Queen seat and a trailer the size of a small cruise liner is where it's at; to others, a stripped-down, matt-black Sportster with performance cams, carb and pipes is the only way a Harley should look.

That's the beauty of Harleys – each one is different and they are very rarely uninteresting.

Page 24: *Custom paintwork and extra chrome typify the approach of most Harley owners to customizing their motorcycles. The work ranges from very good (in this case) to very tacky.*

Page 25, above: *With this many extra running lights the battery will have a hard time putting out enough juice. The two-bar suggests a similarly decked-out trailer somewhere in existence.*

Page 25 below: *This is the other approach to customizing – the ratbike. The more junk and dead animals adorning it, the better; this type of customizing requires the maximum amount of grot possible.*

Left: *It started life as some kind of 80 cubic-inch Evolution bike (possibly a Springer Softail) but has transmogrified into a fairly radical hardtail chop. Exhausts are distinctly illegal, but it seems unlikely the owner is too concerned about that.*

Middle left: *This pre-Evo Shovelhead has been customized to within an inch of its life. Gold-plating, engraving, annodizing and special paint make this a stunning example of the customizer's 'art'.*

Bottom left: *Here's an example of how customizing can actually serve a real purpose – this Low Rider has a custom-made sidecar adapted to take a wheelchair and allows the outfit to be controlled from the sidecar. Now that's a clever piece of engineering.*

Right: *This Evo-engined bike has the lot, from a performance carb to annodized pushrod tubes to engraved heads to chromed covers to a leather tool roll. The only things missing are the highway pegs. And it's out in the rain, which proves that not all these heavily customized bikes go around in the back of a truck.*

Below: *Is it a boat? Is it a plane? No, it's an FLHTC Ultra Classic Electra Glide. Another example of custom paint, extra chrome and a host of running lights – the last word in long-distance touring machines.*

Far left: *This extraordinary creation almost defies belief. There is almost no part of this Harley that remains standard and the work that has gone into it is incredible. It may not be to everyone's taste, but you can certainly appreciate the craftsmanship.*

Left: *The retro-look, the art of making a modern (and reliable) Harley look like an old one, is booming at the moment. This Springer is almost brand new, but the image is definitely that of a 1940s machine.*

Below left: *Pretty in Pink? The addition of special paintwork and a few bolt-on chrome covers transforms an ordinary Fat Boy into very distinctive custom bike.*

Top right: *'Live to Ride, Ride to Live' is a favorite slogan of the Harley customizer, and it can be seen in three separate places on this heavily customized Shovelhead.*

Middle right: *The customizer's art plumbs new depths with this trike towing a coffin trailer. Still, it takes all sorts.*

Bottom right: *Leather tassels are as much a part of the custom Harley look as chrome covers or fancy paint. They serve no purpose other than mere decoration.*

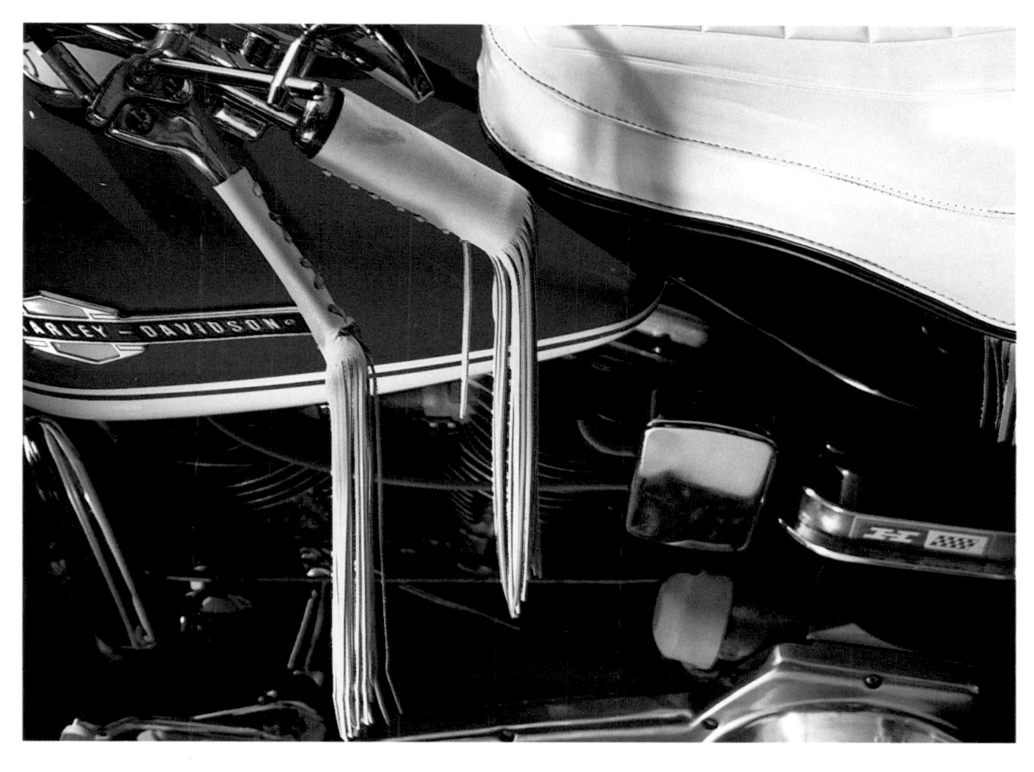

Above: *This Electra Glide has just about everything except the kitchen sink – a host of running lights, acres of chrome trim, leather tassels and much, much more. Known in some circles as the two-wheeled tinsel-truck, the full-dress tourers are usually to be found so bedecked.*

Right: *Yes, it's Joint Effort again. A phenomenal piece of work by any standards, this particular bike is one of the finest examples of a custom Harley-Davidson. It's difficult to imagine the time, skill and patience of the people who built this bike, but the finished product is stunning.*

42 KNUCK
Joint

THE SPORT

Nowadays it's hard to imagine Harley-Davidsons leading the world in motorcycle sport. Harleys have a reputation for being solid, stylish and slow, but this was not always the case. In the past Harleys have enjoyed considerable sporting success, even if it has been in the USA rather than all over the globe.

The first specially-built Harley racer was the 61 cubic-inch, eight-valve twin cam V-twin which was raced with considerable success between 1914 and 1921 in the hands of the 'Wrecking Crew', a team of hotshot racers put together by Harley-Davidson to assure them of race-track success. Factory racing support was dropped at the end of 1921, but Harleys continued to win races in the hands of privateers competing in a variety of events from endurance races and time trials, to flat-track races and hillclimbs.

Racing primarily against their old rivals, Indian, the spirit of competition was fierce and race-track victories were often used in sales literature. The 1930s were a fairly lean time for racing, but after World War II speed records fell to Harley-Davidsons with increasing regularity. In hill-climbing circles Windy Lindstrom became a legend on his almost-stock 45 and 74 cubic-inch Harleys.

In the 1950s Harleys had to work a little harder for sporting success as increasingly competitive machinery arrived from Europe. Indian was now on the verge of collapse so it was up to Harley-Davidson to fly the flag on race-tracks around America. At this time it was the KR750 that was the lynchpin of Harley's racing success, particularly on the dirt-tracks where its handling was less compromised than on the road circuits. The KR was fast, but difficult to ride, and such racers as Cal Rayborn and Mert Lawill made their names on the KR during the '50s and '60s. During the 17 years that the KR raced on American tracks, it won the AMA championship 12 times.

But it was the 1970s that were really the heyday of Harley-Davidson's racing. The XR750, the replacement for the KR, swept all before it on the dirt tracks even if road-racing victories seemed a little harder to come by. In the hands of Jay Springsteen the XR was all-conquering on the dirt, and has only recently been bettered by works Hondas. In road-racing Walter Villa and Cal Rayborn achieved some success on Aermacchi/Harleys, the RR250s and 350s, but real road-racing success eluded them.

By the 1980s the Japanese had a stranglehold on most aspects of motorcycle sport, leaving Harley-Davidson to compete on the drag-strips and on the dirt-tracks. H-D built the XR1000 in the early '80s to compete in Battle of the Twins racing, and in the hands of the multitalented Jay Springsteen, actually won the 1983 Daytona Twins race, reaching speeds of up to 167mph. But even in Twins racing Harleys have been left behind by the dominance of the Italian factories, which leaves aged XR750s to compete on the half-mile and mile flat-tracks. Rumors still persist about the imminent introduction of multi-valve Harley racing engines, but so far this had been little more than speculation fueled by tantalizing hints from the factory.

Page 32: *Drag racing is one of the few areas of motorcycle sport where Harley-Davidson still race competitively. This radical-looking Harley runs on Nitrous Oxide.*

Page 33, above: *Two of Harley-Davidson's top riders, Jay Springsteen and Scott Parker, compare notes before a recent flat-track meeting.*

Page 33, below: *The great Kenny Roberts, better known for his road race exploits aboard a Yamaha, is seen here on a Harley flat-tracker.*

Above: *Claude Temple, a man who achieved many victories aboard Harleys, and who did much to establish the Harley-Davidson as a performance motorcycle. In 1921 he set the first ever 90mph lap of the Brooklands circuit before going on to build his own racing bike using Harley running gear.*

Right: *Jay Springsteen was National Champion in the USA three years running from 1976 to 1978 aboard a Harley-Davidson, and even now he is still riding Harleys and is still competitive.*

Below: *Scott Parker was the 1990 National Champion in the USA and is seen here practising for a Camel Pro National meeting.*

Below right: *Scott Parker in earlier years, even then flying the Harley-Davidson flag aboard an XR750.*

Left: *Harley-Davidson XR750s have been winning flat-track races since they were introduced in the early 1970s and have even won a few road races in their day. Here we see Chris Carr, another famous name from the Harley-Davidson racing stable, riding an XR750 as it was designed to be ridden.*

Below: *A closer look at Scott Parker's XR750 shows a bike that has changed little in 20 years and yet still regularly beats the Japanese opposition. The XR is, without doubt, the most successful dirt-track bike of all time.*

Right: *The XR750 uses aluminum-alloy heads and barrels, and the engine puts out something in the region of 90 horsepower at the back wheel. With no front brake and a top speed well in excess of 100mph, the XR is a fearsome bike to ride.*

Middle right: *It may say Harley-Davidson on the tank, but the engine is an Austrian Rotax and the forks are Japanese Showas. Not that it really matters as long as it wins (and win they often do).*

Bottom: *But it's not all dirt-track racing with Harley-Davidsons. This is an 80 cubic-inch Pro-Stock machine preparing for a run down the strip. The huge potential for tuning what is basically an over-engineered engine means that serious power and torque can be obtained from these big-capacity twins.*

Chart

THE OWNERS

Part of the appeal of Harley-Davidsons is camaraderie of fellow enthusiasts. Although all bikers feel a certain bond of an interest shared, Harley owners seem to have a particularly strong bond with other Harley owners. The Harley Owners Group, HOG, is the biggest motorcycle club in the world with more than 80,000 members worldwide, and more than 300,000 Harley-riding bikers turned up at the 1990 Sturgis rally. That's the sort of loyalty this motorcycle commands.

But while Harley owners get together in groups all over the world, there are two events that are given over 100 percent to Harleys and Harley riders – Cycle Week in Daytona, Florida, and the Black Hills Classic in Sturgis, South Dakota. Cycle Week is ostensibly for the purpose of racing motorcycles, but 90 percent of the people who arrive every year in the spring are there to get together with other Harley folk and have a good time. Few of them ever get to see a race. Riding your bike on Daytona beach and hanging out in the Boot Hill Saloon are what Cycle Week is really about, and tens of thousands of Harley riders turn up to do just that.

For many riders Cycle Week marks the beginning of the riding year. It is held in early spring and for many Harley riders, some of whom arrive towing their bikes on trailers, it is the first outing after the winter and the first chance to show off the winter rebuilds and restorations. Official factory presence is strong at Daytona, with new bikes and merchandise on view to an eager public.

At Sturgis every year there is not even the pretence of watching the racing. People flock from all over the world to the small town of Sturgis just to indulge in a week of nothing but Harleys. In 1990, the 50th anniversary of the Black Hills Classic, upwards of 300,000 people poured into town. Bands play, competitions are run, beer is drunk, hot dogs are eaten and bare flesh is exposed. They called it the biggest biker party ever, and that would seem to be no exaggeration.

It all started back in 1938 when only 1000 people turned out, but by the mid-'80s 30,000 people came to Sturgis on their Harleys. With 300,000 in 1990 it was described as 'Woodstock in leather'. There are those who say that the event has now outgrown the town, but while people still ride Harleys, they will always ride them to Sturgis.

And it isn't only the USA that has big Harley rallies. Europe, Australia and even Japan all have their own Harley gatherings. The European Harley Super-Rally is one of the largest attracting several thousand Harleys and considerably more people every year. In fact, wherever two or more Harleys get together in one place it seems that others invariably follow and crowds gather.

Page 38: *Harley owners getting together, be it at Sturgis, Daytona or anywhere else, seem to become much more than just a bunch of bikers meeting up. The atmosphere makes it something special.*

Page 39, above: *Togetherness the Harley way on Daytona beach.*

Page 39 below: *Meanwhile, the town of Daytona is given over to motorcycling for Speed Week. Although there is plenty of racing to watch, most Harley riders spend the week cruising along the beach or hanging out in the numerous bars with other like-minded enthusiasts.*

Top: *The Harley Owners Group is one of the biggest motorcycle clubs in the world. They organize massive events for their members all over the globe and have a very high profile at the big Harley gatherings.*

Middle: *For instance, here's the official flag of the New York State third annual HOG rally. These people take their get-togethers very seriously indeed.*

Bottom: *And if you don't fancy riding your bike, why not kit your truck out to let everyone know your taste in motorcycles?*

Above: *Just a small selection of the hundreds of thousands of bikes that attended the 50th Black Hills Classic (more commonly known as Sturgis). With around 300,000 people in town for the event, it was described as 'Woodstock in Leather.'*

Right: *Blue jeans and black leather are all part of the Harley image. So is sitting around drinking beer and talking about Harleys with your buddies.*

UBLE
RKING
ONLY
BOOT
SA

EXIT
ONLY
QUALIFIER

Page 42-3: *A Shovelhead motor within a hardtail frame, outside the famous Boot Hill Saloon.*

Left: *Before it became a municipal refuse dump this motorcycle was once a Knucklehead Harley-Davidson. The ratbike as an art-form? Maybe not, but it's certainly the most extensive collection of trash in the western hemisphere.*

Below: *Blue skies, warm sunshine, and a collection of Harleys . . . it has the makings of a good day.*

Above: *The boys are back in town. Part of the attraction of large gatherings of Harleys and Harley folk is cruising up and down Main Street looking cool and checking out the action. Of course nobody notices because they're all doing the same thing, but it's traditional.*

Right: *Although Harley riders are all individualists, there is a strict dress code that has to be conformed to – this is it.*

Left: *At night the constant parade down Main Street continues. Those who aren't in bars drinking beer, or out riding up and down Main Street, sit back and watch the world go by.*

Below: *All through the night the party goes on, with no let up in the comings and goings of the Harley riders. Sturgis is one great big week-long biking party, an event not to be missed by the die-hard Harley fan.*

Right: *It's not just in the USA that large Harley gatherings happen. This is the first HOG European rally which attracted thousands of people – and a lot of rain as well.*

FROM THE TOP OF A 200 FOOT CRANE PLATFORM........
HARLEY-DAVIDSON

THE STARS

The image of the legendary Harley-Davidson has always given it star-appeal. The relative exclusivity and kudos of Harley ownership has attracted celebrities and stars from all areas of music and showbusiness, and this has increased the kudos and added to the legend. Harleys have star quality which in turn attracts the stars.

Stars have been riding and buying Harleys from quite early on, but it was probably Clark Gable who became the first major celebrity to ride a Harley. Since then most of the big names have been seen on, if not actually owned or ridden, Harleys. From Marlene Dietrich to Billy Idol, most of them have at one time or another appeared on a Harley. Elvis was a dedicated Harley fan and owner, Dan Aykroyd led John Belushi's funeral cortege on his Harley, Billy Idol ended up in hospital after crashing his Harley, Malcolm Forbes gave Elizabeth Taylor a purple Harley, and Evel Knievel rode Harleys in his stunts.

But it's the macho, all-American image of the Harley that has attracted the big names. Arnold Schwarzenegger, Hulk Hogan, Clint Eastwood, Kurt Russell, Sylvester Stallone, Burt Reynolds, Larry Holmes, Muhammad Ali, Steve McQueen, Hershel Walker and many others have all owned Harleys. Musicians on the Harley-owners list include Cher, Lou Reed, Olivia Newton-John, Roy Orbison, Bob Dylan, Willie Nelson and Neil Diamond.

Whether used as a posing tool or simply as a means of escaping from the pressures of fame, the Harley has become almost an essential part of a star's wardrobe. It has a style and panache all of its own, something most celebrities hope applies to them as well as their motorcycle. But it's not only stars of stage and screen that own Harleys. Wayne Gardner, a recent 500cc road-racing Grand Prix champion, is an aficionado of the marque. The late Malcolm Forbes, publishing magnate and collector of 'capitalist tools', had a large collection of Harleys and even owned a Harley-Davidson hot-air balloon. Peter de Savary, the British property millionaire, has several Harleys and hosts a large annual Harley rally at his stately home in Berkshire, England. From US senators to British lords, Harleys have a universal appeal to those in search of a bike that says something about them as a person.

Page 48: *Sylvester Stallone, star of Rocky, Rocky II, etc, shows off his immaculate taste in jackets and Harleys. He is just one of many Hollywood celebs to take to a Harley-Davidson.*

Page 49, above: *Clark Gable, easily the coolest of all Harley-riding celebs, is seen here in the 1940s aboard a side-valve Harley.*

Page 49, below: *Mickey Rourke rides a Harley, too, although his riding attire might get him a few strange glances in the Boot Hill Saloon.*

Above: *Although as far as anyone knows Ronnie never rode a Harley, he's seen here picking out a little something for Nancy to wear down on the range.*

Above right: *With a Rebel Yell . . . Billy Idol, rock star and wild boy, recently crashed his Harley, breaking his leg badly. Despite protests from his record company he bought another one when he got out of hospital. He's seen here during Love Ride IV in aid of muscular dystrophy sufferers.*

Below right: *The film that spawned a thousand choppers –* Easy Rider *was all about freedom and the biker lifestyle. It featured Dennis Hopper and Peter Fonda on their Harleys and helped the Harley name on its way into legend.*

HARLEY-

Right and below: *Another film that fueled the Harley-Davidson cult was* Electra Glide in Blue. *All about a patrolman who sought to become a detective, it achieved the same sort of status as* Easy Rider *and made the Electra Glide a household name.*

Left: *It's not just film stars and musicians who own Harleys, either. Those involved in big business, such as Peter de Savary, ride Harleys and he hosts a large annual Harley gathering at his stately home in Berkshire, England.*

Below: *A keen Harley fan relaxes at Daytona.*

THE LOOK

It is curious that while every Harley owner spends so much time and money making their bikes individual, all the owners end up looking the same. This may be a rather sweeping generalization, but there is definitely a Harley 'look' that is strictly adhered to by many Harley riders. It's all part of the Harley scene, and woebetide any Harley rider who doesn't conform.

Actually, there are several 'looks': the outlaw, the CHiPs, and the touring. The outlaw 'look' requires long hair, a beard, tattoos and cut-offs; the CHiPs 'look' demands a Brando-style or Highway Patrol jacket, a CHiPs helmet, and Levis; the touring 'look' needs full-face helmets, his-and-hers matching leathers and a shaggy grey beard. Sunglasses and engineer boots are essential for all.

But where Harley-Davidson have been very clever is in the merchandising. Each 'look' is well catered for in Harley-Davidson's catalogs, enabling the Harley owner to kit out himself (or herself) from head to toe on the 'look' of their choice. Riding gear of every possible type is featured in their clothing catalog, from leather chaps to waterproof oversuits. You can get a dozen different types of leather jacket, half-a-dozen styles of crash-helmet, denims and denim-jackets, a dozen types of riding boot, leather gloves, belts, shirts, leather skirts and waistcoats.

There is even an extensive collection of Harley-Davidson leisurewear that includes over 20 different types of sunglasses, kids clothing, jewelry, watches, baseball caps and just about everything else you could think of. You can buy official Harley money boxes, telephones, underwear, beach towels, bar mats, beer mugs and even removable tattoos.

But it is probably the Harley T-shirts that constitute the single biggest area of related merchandising. You can get T-shirts that say everything and anything about Harleys. From 'God Rides a Harley' to 'If you don't ride a Harley you ain't shit', the sentiments are many and varied. All, however are fiercely pro-Harley and many are also fiercely patriotic. T-shirts saying 'I own a Harley, not just a T-shirt' have become more popular as Harley-branded merchandise makes its way in ever-increasing numbers on to the fashion market. But perhaps the thing that sums it all up best is the T-shirt that says: 'Harley-Davidson – If I have to explain, you wouldn't understand'.

Page 54: *Would you buy a used Harley-Davidson from this man? Only if he absolutely insisted. Headgear may not be out of a Harley clothing catalog, but it certainly says something about the wearer. The beard, however, is a genuine Harley accessory.*

Page 55 above: *As befits a club such as the Harley Owners Group, chapters exist in many and varied locations.*

Page 55 below: *Tattoos are another part of the essential Harley look, but nose-jewelry is optional.*

Right: *Merchandise bearing the Harley name sells well to owners and wannabees alike.*

Below: *These days Harley-Davidson probably make as much money selling T-shirts, and the rights to sell T-shirts, as they do from selling motorcycles. All over the world Harley T-shirts abound.*

Above: *Insignia of various types spell out to those who don't know that the wearer is an owner (or a fan) of Harley-Davidson motorcycles. Patriotism plays a large part in this, with the American Bald Eagle playing a major role in many badges, T-shirts and other merchandise. And it seems that the more badges you wear, the bigger the enthusiast you are.*

Below right: *Yes, you can even get Harley-Davidson pinball machines, as well as beer, clothing and removable tattoos.*

Left: *The archetypal Harley-Davidson rider image. The uniform is spot-on, from the biker shades to the beard to the tattoos and the death's-head jewelry.*

Below: *A more conventional Mr and Mrs H-D look. Note the T-shirt and the abundance of Harley-Davidson badges, patches and other insignia. This look is usually to be found on couples riding full-dress Tour Glides.*

Top right: *In the absence of serious facial hair, a matt black helmet and wrap-round sunglasses must be worn, along with a suitably mean expression.*

Top far right: *Patriotism and Harleys go hand in hand, but no one says that the patriotism has to be for the USA. Here a Scottish Harley rider pins his colors firmly to his Hog.*

Bottom right: *Another traditional Harley look, although as yet they don't seem to make biker sunglasses and crash helmets specifically for canines.*

Bottom far right: *Fun for all the family – shopping at your local Harley dealer can equip you with a whole range of stuff, all bearing the Harley name.*

MOTOR
HARLEY-DAVIDSON
CYCLES
MOTOR
HARLEY-DAVIDSON
CYCLES
Low Rider

Left: *No matter how old the rider, a good pair of sunglasses is the most essential piece of riding gear. Even at night or in the pouring rain a Harley rider is expected to keep his sunglasses on (presumably in case someone recognizes him).*

Above: *A good hat is another essential part of the Harley look. Anything from a stetson to a racoon-skin will do, but a leather confederate soldier's cap is one of the most popular. It goes particularly well with the mirrored sunglasses and the Nick Nolte look.*

Left: *Shop windows in Daytona display just a small selection of the patches that you can buy to show your allegiance to Harley-Davidson. Whoever put the Honda and Kawasaki patches in on the bottom row obviously had a highly-developed sense of fun.*

Below: *This silver belt buckle is a minor work of art, as well as bearing the name of the world's greatest motorcycle manufacturer on it. It's just one of several dozen that you can find at any Harley gathering.*

Above right: *Looking for further Harley adornments is all part and parcel of attending Harley rallies – the more obscure the patch or badge, the better.*

Right: *The work that goes into some of the Harley-related patches can be quite impressive. This jacket, for example . . .*

MOTOR
HARLEY-DAVIDSON
CYCLES
motörhead
England
HARLEY

INDEX

ACKNOWLEDGMENTS

The publisher would like to thank the following for their help in the preparation of this book: Design 23, Helen Dawson for the index, Veronica Price and Nicki Giles for production, Rita Longabucco for picture research and Judith Millidge for editing it.

We are grateful to the following individuals and agencies for permission to use the photographs on the pages noted below.

Bettmann Archive pages 49 top, 50.
Bison Picture Library page 51 below.
Kel Edge pages 33 top, 35 below left, 36 both, 37 top pair.
Tom Isitt page 37 bottom
Bob Jones pages 13 top, 15 below, 25 below, 26 bottom pair, 28 top left, 39 both, 40 bottom, 41 below, 42-3, 45 both, 53 below, 58 both, 59 bottom left, 61, 62, 63 below.
Andrew Morland page 2-3.
National Film Institute page 52 both.
N E Stock/Brian Lance Carr pages 7 top, 28 below.
N E Stock/Ira Cohen pages 13 below, 56 both, 57 below.
N E Stock/Garry Mirando pages 5, 10 below, 21 bottom, 29 bottom.
National Motor Museum Beaulieu page 34 top
Albert Ortega pages 48, 49 below, 51 top.
Tom Riles 33 below.
Bert Shepard/Silver Shutter page 35 right pair.
Garry Stuart pages 1, 2, 4, 6, 7 below, 8-9, 10 top, 11, 12, 14 both, 15 top, 16, 17, 18, 19, 20 both, 21 top, 22 top 3, 23 top pair, 24, 25 top, 26 top, 27 top, 28 top right, 29 top pair, 30, 31, 38, 41 top, 44 both, 46 both, 47 both, 53 top, 55 both, 59 top pair & bottom right, 60, 63.
Carl Vaccarino pages 21 below, 26 below, 40 top pair, 57 top pair, 62 below.